Copyright © 2023 by Connor A. Anderson (Author)

All rights reserved. No part of this book may be reproduced or utilized in any form or by any means, electronic or mechanical, including photocopying, recording or by any information storage and retrieval system, without permission in writing from the publisher, except for brief quotations in critical articles or reviews.

The content of this book is based on various sources and is intended for educational and entertainment purposes only. While the author has made every effort to ensure the accuracy, completeness, and reliability of the information provided, the information may be subject to errors, omissions, or inaccuracies. Therefore, the author makes no warranties, express or implied, regarding the content of this book.

Readers are advised to seek the guidance of a licensed professional before attempting any techniques or actions outlined in this book. The author is not responsible for any losses, damages, or injuries that may arise from the use of information contained within. The information provided in this book is not intended to be a substitute for professional advice, and readers should not rely solely on the information presented.

By reading this book, readers acknowledge that the author is not providing legal, financial, medical, or professional advice. Any reliance on the information contained in this book is solely at the reader's own risk.

Thank you for selecting this book as a valuable source of knowledge and inspiration. Our aim is to provide you with insights and information that will enrich your understanding and enhance your personal growth. We appreciate your decision to embark on this journey of discovery with us, and we hope that this book will exceed your expectations and leave a lasting impact on your life.

Title: Medieval to Renaissance Sports
Subtitle: From Jousts to Javelins: Athletic Pursuits in the Age of Chivalry

Series: Sports Through Time: A Comprehensive History
Author: Connor A. Anderson

Table of Contents

Introduction 6

The shifting landscape of sports in the medieval and Renaissance periods 6

Societal context shaping athletic pursuits 10

Sporting chivalry and ideals of knighthood 14

Chapter 1: The Age of Tournaments 18

Emergence of tournaments as spectacles 18

Jousting and its role in chivalric culture 22

The evolution of tournament rules and formats 26

Chapter 2: Archery and the Longbow 30

Archery as a vital medieval skill 30

The significance of the longbow in warfare and sport ... 33

Archery contests and their cultural importance 36

Chapter 3: Fencing and Duels 40

Development of fencing techniques and schools 40

Duels as displays of honor and skill 44

Influence of fencing on modern combat sports 47

Chapter 4: The Renaissance Humanism and Athletics 51

The revival of interest in ancient Greek and Roman games 51

Humanist ideals and their impact on sports 55

Integration of athleticism with intellectual pursuits 59

Chapter 5: Royal Sports and Hunting 63

Hunting as a royal pastime 63

Falconry, boar hunting, and other noble pursuits 67

Connection between hunting and medieval courtly culture 70

Chapter 6: Martial Arts and Combat Sports 73

Martial arts in medieval Europe and the Far East 73

Unarmed combat techniques and training 77

The fusion of martial arts with cultural traditions 81

Chapter 7: Festivals, Pageantry, and Sports 85

Festivals as platforms for sports and games 85

Theatrical sports and mock battles 89

Symbolism and social function of festive athletics 93

Conclusion 97

The enduring legacy of chivalry and honor in sports 97

The role of medieval and Renaissance sports in shaping modern ideals 101

Reflecting on the evolution from medieval contests to modern athletics 105

Wordbook 109

Supplementary Materials 115

Introduction
The shifting landscape of sports in the medieval and Renaissance periods

Sports, as we understand them today, have a rich and complex history that stretches back centuries. To appreciate the evolution of sports and their profound impact on society, we must embark on a journey through the medieval and Renaissance periods. These eras, marked by dramatic changes in culture, politics, and technology, witnessed a transformation in athletic pursuits that mirrored the shifting societal landscape.

Medieval Beginnings

Our exploration begins in the medieval period, a time when Europe was characterized by feudalism, chivalry, and a distinct social hierarchy. In this feudal system, the nobility and clergy held power, and sports were often the domain of the elite. Yet, even in this rigid structure, sports played a vital role in defining the values and ideals of the age.

Chivalry and Athletic Virtue

Central to medieval sports was the concept of chivalry. Knights and nobles saw athletic prowess as an essential component of their identity, intertwining physical skill with honor, valor, and courtly love. Tournaments emerged as grand spectacles that showcased the physical prowess and courage of knights, while jousting became the ultimate test of chivalric virtue. We delve into the elaborate pageantry of these tournaments, exploring how they epitomized the ideals of knighthood and the code of honor.

Archery: Skill and War

In contrast to the grandeur of tournaments, archery represented a practical and essential skill of the medieval period. The mastery of the longbow, in particular, transformed archers into formidable forces on the battlefield. We unravel the significance of archery in warfare and sport, shedding light on archery contests as cultural touchstones that celebrated precision and discipline.

Fencing and the Duel

Another facet of medieval sports was the art of fencing and dueling. As martial combat evolved, so did the techniques and schools of fencing. Duels, though often fueled by personal vendettas, were also displays of skill and honor. This chapter uncovers the development of fencing techniques, the codes of conduct governing duels, and the enduring influence of fencing on modern combat sports.

The Renaissance Renaissance Humanism and Athletics

Our journey through the shifting landscape of sports then takes us to the Renaissance, a period of intellectual and cultural awakening. Humanism, with its focus on the revival of classical knowledge, profoundly influenced the world of sports. We explore how the rediscovery of ancient Greek and Roman games ignited a passion for athleticism, blending physical prowess with intellectual pursuits.

Royal Sports and Hunting

The Renaissance wasn't just about intellectual pursuits; it was also an age of opulence and royal extravagance. We delve into the world of royal sports, where hunting held a place of paramount importance. Falconry, boar hunting, and other noble pursuits weren't merely pastimes but expressions of power and status. Through these pursuits, we gain insights into the intersection of hunting, courtly culture, and medieval nobility.

Martial Arts and Cultural Fusion

As we progress, we encounter the fascinating world of martial arts and combat sports. Beyond Europe, martial arts flourished both in the Far East and on the continent. This chapter explores the development of unarmed combat techniques and the fusion of martial arts with cultural traditions, shedding light on their lasting impact.

Festivals, Pageantry, and Social Function

Our journey concludes with a look at festivals, pageantry, and sports as expressions of communal identity.

These events weren't mere spectacles; they were theatrical performances and mock battles rich in symbolism and social function. We uncover the significance of festive athletics and how they mirrored the values and aspirations of medieval and Renaissance societies.

In this exploration of the shifting landscape of sports, we will unravel the threads that connect medieval chivalry to Renaissance humanism, archery to warfare, and martial arts to cultural fusion. Join us as we step into the past, where sports were more than games; they were reflections of the ever-changing world they inhabited.

Societal context shaping athletic pursuits

To truly understand the evolution of sports during the medieval and Renaissance periods, it is imperative to delve deep into the societal context that not only influenced but also defined the athletic pursuits of the time. Sports, in these eras, were not isolated activities; they were integral components of the intricate tapestry of medieval and Renaissance societies. This chapter will illuminate the multifaceted ways in which societal norms, values, and structures shaped athletic endeavors during this transformative period.

Feudalism and the Role of the Nobility

The feudal system, dominant during the medieval era, was a hierarchical structure that significantly impacted the practice of sports. At its apex were monarchs and nobles who held sway over vast lands and vast resources. Sports were often a prerogative of the nobility, a means to both display their prowess and reinforce their status. Tournaments, jousting, and hunting were not merely leisure activities but displays of chivalric virtue and power. We will explore how these activities were intertwined with the feudal system, reinforcing the social hierarchy and ideals of knighthood.

Religion and Morality

Religion, a cornerstone of medieval life, also influenced the practice of sports. The Church played a pivotal role in shaping societal norms and values, and its moral codes extended to the realm of sports. Certain forms of competition and leisure were frowned upon or even prohibited due to perceived moral implications. Yet, in a paradoxical twist, some sports were embraced and even championed by the Church. We will delve into the complex relationship between religion and sports, shedding light on the moral boundaries that defined athletic pursuits.

Gender and Class Distinctions

Medieval and Renaissance societies were marked by rigid gender and class distinctions. Sports, too, were subject to these divisions. While men of nobility often had the opportunity to participate in prestigious tournaments, women faced considerable limitations in their sporting endeavors. The lower classes had their own forms of recreational activities, often tied to rural life and communal celebrations. This chapter will explore the gender and class dynamics of sports during this era, highlighting both the constraints and opportunities that individuals faced based on their social standing.

Technology and Sporting Equipment

Technological advancements, although comparatively modest by modern standards, played a significant role in shaping the sports of the medieval and Renaissance periods. The introduction of the longbow, for instance, revolutionized archery and had profound implications for warfare and sport alike. Likewise, innovations in armor design influenced the nature of jousting tournaments. We will examine how technological developments influenced the equipment and rules of sports, giving rise to new forms of competition and spectacle.

Urbanization and Communal Sports

The gradual shift from rural agrarian societies to urban centers in the late medieval and Renaissance periods had far-reaching effects on sports. Urbanization fostered the growth of communal spaces, paving the way for organized sports and games within city walls. Festivals and public gatherings became opportunities for sports, and new forms of entertainment emerged. This chapter will illuminate how the migration of populations to urban centers transformed the landscape of sports, giving rise to more diverse and accessible athletic pursuits.

Conclusion: A Tapestry of Influence

As we navigate the intricate web of societal factors that shaped athletic pursuits in the medieval and

Renaissance periods, we uncover a tapestry of influence. Feudalism, religion, gender roles, technology, and urbanization all left their indelible marks on the world of sports. Together, these elements forged the unique sporting traditions of the time, reflecting the values, aspirations, and challenges of societies in flux. In the following chapters, we will explore specific sports and their evolution within this rich socio-cultural backdrop, offering a comprehensive view of the dynamic relationship between sports and society during this transformative period.

Sporting chivalry and ideals of knighthood

In the medieval and Renaissance periods, the concept of chivalry was not confined to the battlefield or the courts of nobility; it permeated every aspect of life, including the realm of sports. Chivalry was more than a code of conduct for knights; it was a philosophy that championed honor, virtue, and noble ideals. This chapter delves into the profound influence of chivalry on athletic pursuits, exploring how sports became a stage where knights and nobles displayed their commitment to these lofty principles.

Chivalry: The Code of the Noble Warrior

At the heart of chivalry was a code of conduct that dictated how knights should behave on and off the battlefield. Loyalty to one's lord, courage in the face of danger, and the protection of the weak were fundamental tenets. But chivalry was not merely a set of rules; it was a way of life. Knights were expected to embody these principles in their every action. This chapter will explore the core values of chivalry and how they found expression in sports.

Tournaments: A Showcase of Chivalric Virtue

Tournaments, with their elaborate pageantry and displays of martial skill, were the quintessential sporting events of the medieval and Renaissance periods. These grand spectacles were not just contests of physical prowess; they were celebrations of chivalric virtue. Knights jousted not only for victory but also to demonstrate their adherence to the ideals of chivalry. We will uncover how tournaments served as a stage where knights showcased their courage, honor, and commitment to their lords.

The Joust: Chivalry in Action

The joust, a highlight of tournaments, epitomized the essence of chivalry. Knights engaged in combat, armed with lances, striving to unseat their opponents while adhering to a strict code of honor. The joust was more than a competition; it was a ritual of chivalric ideals. This chapter will explore the symbolism and significance of the joust, shedding light on how it epitomized the intersection of sports and chivalry.

Chivalric Ideals and Archery

Archery, another prominent sport of the time, was not exempt from the influence of chivalry. The longbow, a formidable weapon on the battlefield, was also a symbol of honor and skill in sport. Archery contests were more than tests of marksmanship; they were displays of chivalric virtue. This chapter will delve into how archers embodied the values of chivalry through their dedication to precision and discipline.

Fencing and Duels: The Art of Honor

In the realm of fencing and dueling, chivalry was on full display. Knights and nobles engaged in duels not only to settle personal disputes but also to defend their honor and uphold their reputation. The codes of conduct governing duels were deeply rooted in chivalric ideals, emphasizing courage, fairness, and integrity. We will explore how the art of fencing and dueling became arenas where knights and nobles could prove their commitment to the code of chivalry.

Chivalry Beyond the Arena

Chivalry extended beyond sporting events. Knights and nobles sought to live according to its principles in their daily lives. This chapter will touch on how chivalry influenced not only sports but also matters of courtly love, etiquette, and personal conduct, providing a holistic view of its impact on medieval and Renaissance society.

Conclusion: The Legacy of Sporting Chivalry

As we conclude our exploration of sporting chivalry and the ideals of knighthood, we recognize that these concepts were more than superficial decorations on the world of sports. They were the very essence of athletic pursuits during the medieval and Renaissance periods. Through tournaments, jousts, archery contests, fencing, and duels, knights and nobles demonstrated their unwavering commitment to the noble ideals of chivalry. In the following chapters, we will continue to unravel the intricate tapestry of sports in this era, each thread woven with the values and aspirations of a society deeply influenced by chivalry.

Chapter 1: The Age of Tournaments
Emergence of tournaments as spectacles

In the annals of medieval and Renaissance sports, few events captured the imagination and hearts of both participants and spectators like tournaments. These grand spectacles were more than mere contests; they were pageants of chivalry, exhibitions of martial skill, and communal celebrations. This chapter explores the fascinating origins and evolution of tournaments as they emerged from the shadows of battlefield combat to become the dazzling sporting spectacles that defined an era.

The Birth of Tournaments: A Martial Proving Ground

Tournaments trace their origins to the martial training grounds of early medieval Europe. In the tumultuous centuries following the fall of the Western Roman Empire, knights and warriors sought opportunities to hone their combat skills. Jousts and melees, organized as training exercises, provided valuable experience in the art of war. We will delve into the early forms of these martial contests and their transition from practice to public spectacle.

The Transformation of Combat Training

As medieval society stabilized and feudal lords sought to consolidate their power, tournaments began to take on new significance. They evolved from simple training events into complex, highly organized affairs. The role of tournaments shifted from merely preparing knights for battle to showcasing their chivalric virtues and martial prowess to a wider audience. This chapter will examine the factors that drove this transformation, including the influence of chivalry, the growth of feudal courts, and the desire for prestige.

Chivalry on Display: The Tournament as a Pageant of Knighthood

By the 12th and 13th centuries, tournaments had evolved into grand pageants of chivalry. Knights and nobles participated not only to demonstrate their martial skills but also to display their adherence to the ideals of knighthood. Elaborate armor, heraldry, and codes of conduct were central to these events. We will explore how tournaments became platforms for knights to showcase their courage, honor, and loyalty, emphasizing the inseparable link between chivalry and these sporting extravaganzas.

Tournament Formats and Variations

Tournaments were not uniform events; their formats and rules varied across regions and time periods. Some tournaments focused on jousting, where knights faced each other in one-on-one combat, while others favored larger melees, where teams clashed in mock battles. The rules and objectives of tournaments also evolved over time. This chapter will provide an in-depth look at the diverse forms and rules of tournaments, highlighting the skills and strategies required for success.

The Spectacle of Tournaments: A Multisensory Experience

Attending a tournament was a multisensory experience that engaged all aspects of medieval and Renaissance life. The thundering hooves of charging horses, the clash of weapons, the colorful banners, and the cheers of the crowd created a vibrant atmosphere that transcended mere sport. We will immerse ourselves in the sensory richness of tournaments, from the acrid smell of sweat-soaked armor to the taste of victory and defeat.

The Enduring Allure of Tournaments

Tournaments remained a fixture of medieval and Renaissance culture for centuries, evolving in response to changing times. While their prominence waned as the Renaissance gave way to the modern era, the legacy of tournaments endures in modern sports and entertainment. This chapter will conclude by examining how the tradition of tournaments persists in contemporary reenactments, festivals, and sporting events, ensuring that the spirit of chivalry and the spectacle of tournaments continue to captivate audiences today.

Conclusion: Tournaments as Timeless Icons

As we conclude our exploration of the emergence of tournaments as spectacles, we recognize that these events were more than mere competitions; they were symbols of an age defined by chivalry, honor, and martial prowess. Tournaments were the crucibles where knights forged their reputations and tested their mettle. They captured the essence of an era where sports were not just pastimes but reflections of a society's values and aspirations. In the following chapters, we will continue our journey through the age of tournaments, exploring their role in shaping the medieval and Renaissance worlds.

Jousting and its role in chivalric culture

In the tapestry of medieval and Renaissance tournaments, few events captured the essence of chivalry and honor more vividly than the joust. This chapter delves into the intricate world of jousting, examining how it emerged as the quintessential chivalric sport and the profound impact it had on the culture and ideals of knighthood during this vibrant era.

The Birth of the Joust: From Martial Exercise to Spectacle of Courage

The origins of jousting can be traced back to the early Middle Ages when knights engaged in mounted combat exercises as part of their training regimen. These contests gradually evolved from practical martial training into public spectacles. We will explore the transition of the joust from a martial exercise to a dazzling display of chivalric virtues, where knights proved their mettle and showcased their loyalty and courage.

The Joust as a Test of Valor and Honor

At the heart of jousting lay the concept of personal valor and honor. Knights entered the lists not only to win glory but also to defend their honor and that of their lords. The chivalric code demanded that knights adhere to strict rules of conduct, emphasizing courtesy, fair play, and respect for opponents. This chapter will delve into the intricate code of chivalry that governed the joust, highlighting its role in promoting virtue and noble ideals.

The Jousting Tournament: Pageantry and Symbolism

Jousting tournaments were more than just contests of skill; they were extravagant displays of pageantry and symbolism. Elaborate armor, heraldry, and banners adorned the jousters, each element carrying deep significance. We will unravel the layers of symbolism in jousting tournaments, showcasing how they became platforms for knights to communicate their identities, allegiances, and values to a wide audience.

The Mechanics of the Joust: Lance, Horse, and Skill

To truly appreciate the art of jousting, one must understand its mechanics. We will dissect the jousting match, from the selection of horses and the design of lances to the techniques employed by knights. The joust demanded not only physical skill but also an intimate understanding of the physics of combat. Through detailed descriptions and accounts, we will bring to life the excitement and tension of the jousting field.

Jousting's Influence on Chivalric Culture

Jousting had a profound influence on the broader chivalric culture of the medieval and Renaissance periods. It shaped notions of honor, courage, and valor, becoming a metaphor for the knightly virtues celebrated in literature and art. We will explore how the imagery and ideals of the joust permeated medieval romances, poetry, and visual arts, leaving an indelible mark on the collective imagination.

The Decline of the Joust: Legacy and Endurance

As we journey through the rise of jousting, we will also examine its eventual decline. The transition from medieval chivalry to the early modern period brought changes in warfare and society, leading to a waning interest in the joust. However, the legacy of jousting endured, finding new life in historical reenactments, literature, and modern entertainment.

Conclusion: The Joust as a Timeless Emblem of Chivalry

The joust was more than a sporting event; it was a reflection of the chivalric ideals that defined an age. It celebrated valor, honor, and loyalty while providing knights with a stage to demonstrate their mettle. As we conclude our exploration of jousting and its role in chivalric culture, we recognize it as a timeless emblem of an era when sports were not merely contests but also powerful expressions of the virtues that shaped a society. In the following chapters, we will continue to unveil the rich tapestry of tournaments in the medieval and Renaissance periods.

The evolution of tournament rules and formats

In the vibrant tapestry of medieval and Renaissance tournaments, rules and formats played a pivotal role in shaping the nature of these grand spectacles. As we delve into the evolution of tournament rules and formats, we discover the intricate interplay between tradition and innovation, safety and spectacle, and chivalry and competition.

Early Tournaments: Informal and Chaotic Origins

The earliest tournaments in the medieval period were often informal affairs, lacking standardized rules and formats. Knights gathered for combat exercises and friendly competitions, and the events could be chaotic and dangerous. We will journey back to these early tournaments, examining how they laid the foundation for the structured tournaments that would follow.

Emergence of Formal Regulations: Codifying the Chivalric Sport

As tournaments gained popularity and prominence, the need for formal regulations became apparent. Knights and nobles began to codify rules governing everything from the conduct of participants to the adjudication of victors. This chapter will explore the emergence of these formal regulations, revealing how they reflected the ideals of chivalry and the desire to transform tournaments into displays of honor and virtue.

Jousts and Melees: The Two Pillars of Tournaments

Tournaments encompassed a variety of contests, with jousts and melees emerging as the two primary pillars. Jousting, a one-on-one mounted combat, and melees, team-based mock battles, offered distinct challenges and required different skill sets. We will dissect the rules and formats of both jousts and melees, examining how they evolved in response to changes in weaponry, armor, and tactics.

Lances, Weapons, and Armor: Evolving for Safety and Spectacle

The safety of participants and spectators was a paramount concern as tournaments evolved. Innovations in weaponry and armor aimed to strike a balance between spectacle and security. Jousting lances, for instance, were designed to break upon impact, reducing the risk of injury. Armor also underwent transformations to provide protection while allowing for greater mobility. This chapter will delve into the technological advancements that influenced tournament safety.

Adjudication and Scoring: Balancing Fair Play and Spectacle

The determination of victors in tournaments required careful adjudication. A panel of judges, often including heralds and experienced knights, played a crucial role in assessing the outcome of matches. We will explore the scoring systems, methods of adjudication, and the challenges of maintaining fairness and impartiality in an environment where honor was at stake.

Variations and Regional Differences: A Diverse Landscape of Tournaments

Tournaments were not uniform across regions and time periods. Different cultures and locales embraced variations in rules and formats. Some tournaments incorporated specific rituals, while others introduced unique challenges. We will examine the diversity of tournaments, highlighting regional variations that added richness to the tapestry of chivalric sports.

The Decline and Legacy of Tournaments: From Tradition to Modern Reenactment

As we journey through the evolution of tournament rules and formats, we will also explore the factors that contributed to the decline of tournaments in the early modern period. However, the legacy of these events persists in modern reenactments, festivals, and historical studies, keeping alive the spirit of chivalry and the fascination with medieval and Renaissance tournaments.

Conclusion: The Enduring Impact of Tournament Rules and Formats

Tournament rules and formats were not mere guidelines; they were the framework upon which the grand pageantry of chivalric sports was built. Their evolution mirrored the changing times, from informal gatherings to structured spectacles that celebrated honor, courage, and skill. As we conclude our exploration of this aspect of the Age of Tournaments, we recognize the enduring impact of these rules and formats, as they continue to influence the world of sports and recreation today. In the following chapters, we will further unveil the captivating world of medieval and Renaissance tournaments.

Chapter 2: Archery and the Longbow

Archery as a vital medieval skill

In the annals of medieval and Renaissance Europe, few skills were as vital and transformative as archery. This chapter takes aim at the heart of archery, exploring its pivotal role as a skill that transcended sport and warfare, shaping both individual destinies and the course of history.

The Bow as a Weapon of War

Archery was more than a pastime; it was a matter of survival. In an era marked by warfare and conflict, the ability to wield a bow effectively was a crucial skill for both soldiers and hunters. We will delve into the tactical advantages of archery in medieval warfare, where archers played a pivotal role in battles and sieges, and where the longbow would emerge as a game-changer.

The Longbow Revolution: Power and Precision

The longbow, a technological marvel of its time, transformed the landscape of archery. Its design allowed for greater draw weight and power, enabling archers to shoot arrows with remarkable force and accuracy. This chapter will explore the evolution of the longbow, its design innovations, and the advantages it conferred on those who mastered it.

Archers of England: The Yeomen and Their Longbows

England, in particular, embraced the longbow as an emblem of national identity and military prowess. Yeomen, skilled archers from the English countryside, became an essential component of English armies. We will examine the training, discipline, and societal role of these archers, who played a pivotal role in some of the most significant battles in medieval history, including the Hundred Years' War.

Hunting and Survival: Archery Beyond the Battlefield

Archery was not confined to warfare; it was also a means of survival. Hunters relied on their bows to provide food for their families and communities. We will venture into the forests and wilds of medieval Europe, exploring the symbiotic relationship between archery and the sustenance of medieval societies.

Archery Contests: Skill, Prestige, and Cultural Significance

As archery evolved from a practical skill to a revered discipline, contests and competitions emerged to celebrate marksmanship and skill. These contests were not just displays of prowess; they carried cultural and societal significance. This chapter will illuminate how archery contests became platforms for individuals to prove their worth, gain prestige, and even find opportunities for social advancement.

The Symbolism of Archery: Myth, Legend, and Folklore

Archery was more than a practical skill; it held a place of reverence in myth, legend, and folklore. Heroes and heroines, from Robin Hood to the legendary Swiss marksman William Tell, were celebrated for their archery feats. We will journey through the rich tapestry of archery-related stories and their enduring impact on the popular imagination.

Conclusion: Archery's Legacy of Skill and Symbolism

As we conclude our exploration of archery as a vital medieval skill, we recognize its dual nature as a practical necessity and a symbol of precision and discipline. Archery shaped the course of battles, filled the tables of countless families, and inspired legends that continue to captivate hearts and minds. In the following chapters, we will draw our bows and set our sights on the broader landscape of archery, exploring its cultural significance and impact on medieval and Renaissance societies.

The significance of the longbow in warfare and sport

The longbow, a marvel of medieval engineering, stands as a testament to the ingenuity of the era. Its significance extends far beyond the battlefield, encompassing both the realm of warfare and the world of sport. This chapter delves into the multifaceted role of the longbow, exploring how it became an iconic weapon of war and a symbol of precision and skill in sport.

The Longbow's Dominance in Medieval Warfare

The longbow's emergence on the battlefield marked a revolutionary shift in the dynamics of medieval warfare. Its exceptional draw weight and power gave archers the ability to launch arrows with unparalleled force and range. We will explore the tactical advantages that the longbow conferred upon English armies during the Hundred Years' War, with a particular focus on battles like Crécy and Agincourt, where longbowmen played pivotal roles.

The Longbowmen: A Formidable and Feared Force

The men who wielded the longbow, often referred to as longbowmen or archers, were renowned for their skill and discipline. Trained from a young age in the art of archery, these soldiers were a formidable force on the battlefield. This chapter will delve into the training, equipment, and tactics that made longbowmen such an essential component of medieval armies.

Longbows vs. Armor: The Power to Penetrate

One of the longbow's most significant contributions to warfare was its ability to penetrate armor. This feature made it a formidable weapon against heavily armored knights and infantry. We will explore the technical aspects of arrow design and the longbow's effectiveness in countering armor, revealing how it influenced battlefield strategies.

The Longbow in Sport: A Test of Skill and Precision

Beyond its role in warfare, the longbow found its place in the world of sport and competition. Archery contests and tournaments celebrated the skill and precision of archers who wielded the longbow. This chapter will shift gears to explore the cultural and sporting significance of the longbow, examining how it became a symbol of marksmanship and honor in tournaments and competitions.

Archery Contests: A Showcase of Longbow Skill

Archery contests were not just sporting events; they were displays of skill and marksmanship. We will immerse ourselves in the world of archery contests, exploring the rules, formats, and cultural importance of these events. Archers, often yeomen or individuals from various social backgrounds, competed to demonstrate their mastery of the longbow and their adherence to the ideals of chivalry.

The Longbow as a Symbol of Precision and Discipline

The longbow's reputation extended beyond the archery range. It became a symbol of precision, discipline, and skill in medieval and Renaissance society. This chapter will delve into the cultural and symbolic significance of the longbow, examining how it was celebrated in literature, art, and folklore, and how it embodied the values of precision and discipline cherished in the age of chivalry.

Conclusion: The Longbow's Dual Legacy

As we conclude our exploration of the significance of the longbow in warfare and sport, we recognize its dual legacy. It was a weapon that reshaped the course of medieval warfare, enabling English armies to achieve remarkable victories. Simultaneously, it was an emblem of precision, discipline, and honor in the world of sport, leaving an indelible mark on the cultural landscape of the time. In the following chapters, we will continue to uncover the rich tapestry of archery and its enduring impact on medieval and Renaissance societies.

Archery contests and their cultural importance

Archery contests, where skilled archers showcased their precision, discipline, and marksmanship, held a unique place in the cultural landscape of medieval and Renaissance Europe. This chapter delves into the rich tradition of archery competitions, exploring their cultural significance, the rules and formats that governed them, and their impact on society.

A Test of Skill and Precision

Archery contests were more than mere sporting events; they were tests of an archer's skill and precision. Participants competed to demonstrate their ability to hit targets with accuracy, often under challenging conditions. We will explore the technical aspects of archery contests, including the types of targets used, distances, and scoring systems, providing insight into the challenges archers faced.

Archery Guilds and Associations

Archery contests were often organized and regulated by archery guilds and associations. These organizations played a central role in preserving and promoting the sport of archery. We will delve into the structure and functions of archery guilds, their roles in fostering competition, and their contributions to the cultural fabric of medieval and Renaissance society.

Tournaments and Festivals: A Showcase of Archery Skills

Archery contests were not isolated events; they were integrated into larger tournaments and festivals. These gatherings provided a platform for archers to display their talents and for communities to come together in celebration. This chapter will illuminate the role of archery within the broader context of tournaments and festivals, showcasing how it contributed to the pageantry and communal spirit of these occasions.

The Role of Archery in Chivalric Culture

Archery contests were imbued with chivalric ideals. Archers were expected to not only demonstrate their skill but also uphold the principles of honor and fair play. The code of chivalry extended to the archery range, shaping the conduct of competitors and spectators alike. We will explore how archery became a symbol of virtuous competition and adherence to noble values.

The Symbolism of Archery: Folklore and Legends

Archery contests also held a place in folklore and legends, contributing to the rich tapestry of medieval and Renaissance storytelling. Heroes and heroines, often archers of exceptional skill, were celebrated in tales of daring feats and marksmanship. This chapter will journey through the archery-related stories and their enduring impact on the cultural imagination.

Archery as a Social and Community Activity

Participation in archery contests extended beyond individual competition; it was a communal activity that brought people together. Archery ranges served as gathering places, fostering a sense of camaraderie and belonging. We will delve into the social aspects of archery, examining how it created bonds within communities and allowed individuals to showcase their talents.

The Decline and Legacy of Archery Contests

As we explore the cultural importance of archery contests, we will also examine the factors that contributed to their decline in the early modern period. However, the legacy of these contests endures in modern archery traditions, historical reenactments, and the continuing fascination with precision and discipline in marksmanship.

Conclusion: Archery Contests as Cultural Icons

Archery contests, with their emphasis on skill, precision, and honor, were more than just sporting events; they were cultural icons that left an indelible mark on the medieval and Renaissance eras. They celebrated the virtues of discipline and excellence, providing a platform for archers to demonstrate their prowess while upholding the ideals of chivalry. In the following chapters, we will continue to unravel the captivating world of archery and its profound impact on society.

Chapter 3: Fencing and Duels

Development of fencing techniques and schools

The art of fencing, with its precise movements, intricate techniques, and rich history, stands as a testament to the evolution of combat sports and martial arts in medieval and Renaissance Europe. In this chapter, we will immerse ourselves in the world of fencing, tracing the development of techniques and the emergence of fencing schools that laid the foundation for the modern sport.

The Early Roots of Fencing: From Combat to Skill

Fencing traces its origins to the need for combat skills in the medieval and Renaissance periods. Knights and soldiers required proficiency in swordplay, not just for battle but also for personal defense. We will explore the early roots of fencing, where practicality and survival were paramount, and how these foundations evolved into a more structured discipline.

The Italian Masters: Pioneers of Fencing

Italy played a pivotal role in the development of fencing techniques and schools. Italian fencing masters, such as Fiore dei Liberi and Filippo Vadi, documented their knowledge in treatises that laid out the fundamentals of swordsmanship. We will delve into the contributions of these early masters, examining their teachings and their impact on the evolution of fencing.

The Spanish School: Influence on Rapier Fencing

Spain, too, made significant contributions to fencing through the emergence of the Spanish school. The development of the rapier, a slender and agile sword, revolutionized fencing techniques. Spanish masters like Jerónimo Sánchez de Carranza and Luis Pacheco de Narváez advanced the art of rapier fencing. This chapter will explore the unique characteristics of Spanish fencing and its lasting influence.

The Transition to Sport: Foil, Épée, and Sabre

As the Renaissance gave way to the early modern period, fencing began to transition from a martial discipline to a sport. The introduction of weapons like the foil, épée, and sabre transformed the nature of fencing contests. We will examine how these weapons were adapted for sporting purposes and the emergence of rules and conventions that defined competitive fencing.

Fencing Masters and Schools: Bastions of Knowledge

Fencing masters and schools became bastions of knowledge and tradition. These institutions were responsible for preserving and transmitting fencing techniques and principles. We will explore the role of fencing schools in training students, disseminating treatises, and maintaining the integrity of the art of fencing.

The Influence of Fencing on Modern Combat Sports

Fencing's impact extended beyond its own discipline. It influenced the development of modern combat sports and martial arts. The concepts of timing, distance, and strategy that are central to fencing found their way into other martial arts and combat sports. We will examine how fencing left its mark on disciplines like boxing, mixed martial arts, and even stage combat.

Fencing in Literature and Culture: A Symbol of Skill and Honor

Fencing also found its way into literature, art, and culture. Characters skilled in the art of the sword often embodied notions of honor, skill, and valor. We will journey through the representation of fencing in literary works, paintings, and other forms of artistic expression, uncovering its enduring symbolic significance.

Conclusion: The Legacy of Fencing Techniques and Schools

As we conclude our exploration of the development of fencing techniques and schools, we recognize their profound impact on the world of combat sports and martial arts. Fencing evolved from a practical skill into a highly refined discipline, with distinct techniques and traditions that continue to shape modern fencing and martial arts. In the following chapters, we will continue to unravel the intricate world of fencing and dueling in the medieval and Renaissance periods.

Duels as displays of honor and skill

Duels, with their potent blend of personal honor, martial skill, and societal significance, held a distinct place in the cultural landscape of medieval and Renaissance Europe. This chapter delves into the world of dueling, examining how these confrontations became more than mere conflicts but rather showcases of honor and skill.

The Duel's Origins: Feud, Honor, and Resolution

The origins of dueling can be traced to the medieval concept of feuds and honor-bound obligations. Disputes between individuals and families were often resolved through combat. We will explore the historical and cultural contexts that gave rise to the duel, examining how it evolved from a means of settling scores into a structured form of combat.

The Code of Honor: Rules and Etiquette

Duels were governed by a complex code of honor and etiquette. This code prescribed the rules of engagement, the choice of weapons, and the behavior expected of participants. We will delve into the intricacies of the code of honor, exploring how it shaped the conduct and outcomes of duels.

The Dueling Weapons: Rapiers, Swords, and Pistols

The choice of weapons in a duel was a crucial aspect of the confrontation. Different eras and regions favored distinct weapons, from rapiers and swords to pistols. Each weapon required a unique set of skills and techniques. This chapter will examine the significance of dueling weapons and how they influenced the dynamics of duels.

Masters of the Duel: Fencing Schools and Instructors

Mastery of dueling techniques often required training under skilled instructors and within established fencing schools. Fencing masters played a pivotal role in preparing individuals for duels, imparting not only the physical skills but also the principles of honor and discipline. We will explore the role of fencing schools and masters in the world of dueling.

The Spectacle of Duels: Public vs. Private Conflicts

Duels took place in various settings, from secluded locations to public squares, and each setting carried its own implications. Public duels could serve as dramatic displays of honor and courage, while private duels often occurred behind closed doors, settling personal disputes away from the public eye. We will investigate the differing motivations and consequences of public versus private duels.

The Impact of Duels on Society and Culture

Duels had a profound impact on society and culture. They left an indelible mark on literature, art, and popular imagination, often serving as symbols of honor and valor. This chapter will journey through the representation of duels in these cultural forms, highlighting their role in shaping societal ideals.

Decline and Transformation: Duels in the Modern Era

As we explore duels as displays of honor and skill, we will also examine their decline in the modern era. Legal and societal changes led to the gradual waning of dueling as a means of conflict resolution. However, the legacy of duels endures in the codes of honor, martial traditions, and the enduring fascination with these confrontations.

Conclusion: Duels as Timeless Testaments

Duels were more than mere clashes of steel; they were timeless testaments to personal honor, martial skill, and societal values. As we conclude our exploration of duels as displays of honor and skill, we recognize their enduring significance in the annals of medieval and Renaissance culture. In the following chapters, we will continue to unravel the intricate world of fencing and dueling in this vibrant era.

Influence of fencing on modern combat sports

The legacy of fencing, with its precise techniques, strategic thinking, and emphasis on martial skill, extends far beyond its historical roots. This chapter explores how fencing has influenced and contributed to the development of modern combat sports, shaping the way we approach combat and competition in contemporary times.

The Art of Defense: Fencing's Contribution to Boxing

Fencing's emphasis on defensive techniques, footwork, and the concept of distance played a significant role in the evolution of boxing. We will delve into how fencing principles influenced the art of boxing, including the use of guards, parries, and counterattacks, and how these elements transformed boxing into a sophisticated combat sport.

Fencing Footwork: The Foundation of Martial Arts

Fencing's intricate footwork, with its emphasis on balance, agility, and movement, has had a profound impact on martial arts disciplines. This chapter will explore how fencing footwork principles influenced the development of martial arts such as karate, taekwondo, and Brazilian jiu-jitsu, revolutionizing the way combat sports are practiced and taught.

Strategic Thinking: Fencing's Influence on MMA

Fencing's strategic approach to combat, involving the anticipation of opponents' moves and the use of feints and psychological tactics, has influenced modern mixed martial arts (MMA). We will examine how fencing's strategic thinking has shaped the evolution of MMA, with fighters incorporating elements of fencing into their training and competition strategies.

The Fencing Weaponry: Foil, Épée, and Sabre in Modern Sport

Fencing's three primary weapons—the foil, épée, and sabre—have not remained confined to the fencing salle. They have made their way into modern sport, often serving as training tools for athletes in various combat sports. This chapter will explore how these weapons have been adapted and integrated into contemporary combat sports and martial arts training.

The Fencing Mindset: Discipline and Precision in Combat Sports

Fencing's emphasis on discipline, precision, and mental fortitude has transcended its own discipline and become a mindset adopted by athletes in various combat sports. We will delve into how the fencing mindset has influenced fighters and competitors, enhancing their focus, control, and strategic thinking in the heat of combat.

Safety and Sport: Fencing's Contribution to Protective Gear

Fencing's commitment to safety and protective gear has had a broader impact on combat sports. The development of fencing masks, gloves, and protective clothing has served as a model for the creation of safety equipment in other combat sports. This chapter will examine how fencing's dedication to safety has influenced the design and use of protective gear in contemporary martial arts.

Fencing in Popular Culture: A Source of Inspiration

Fencing's elegance, precision, and portrayal of martial skill have made it a source of inspiration in popular culture. We will journey through film, literature, and entertainment, exploring how fencing has been depicted and romanticized, and how it continues to captivate and shape the public perception of combat sports.

Conclusion: Fencing's Enduring Impact on Combat Sports

As we conclude our exploration of the influence of fencing on modern combat sports, we recognize its enduring impact on the way we approach combat, competition, and martial training in contemporary times. Fencing's legacy continues to shape the world of combat sports, providing valuable insights into technique, strategy, and the martial mindset. In the following chapters, we will continue to unravel the intricate world of fencing and dueling in the medieval and Renaissance periods.

Chapter 4: The Renaissance Humanism and Athletics

The revival of interest in ancient Greek and Roman games

The Renaissance period marked a reawakening of intellectual curiosity and a deep appreciation for the classical civilizations of ancient Greece and Rome. This chapter explores how the Renaissance Humanism movement played a pivotal role in the revival of interest in ancient Greek and Roman games, igniting a passion for the physical pursuits of antiquity.

Humanism and the Rediscovery of Antiquity

Renaissance Humanism, with its emphasis on the study of classical texts and the values of human potential and achievement, served as a catalyst for the revival of ancient Greek and Roman culture. We will delve into the core principles of Humanism and how they inspired a thirst for knowledge about the past.

The Influence of Ancient Greece: The Olympic Games

The Olympic Games of ancient Greece, with their celebration of physical prowess and the ideal of the balanced individual, became a focal point of interest during the Renaissance. We will explore how the rediscovery of ancient Greek texts and the works of scholars like Pausanias and

Philostratus fueled a fascination with the Olympic Games and their cultural significance.

Roman Sporting Culture: Gladiatorial Combat and More

The Romans, too, left a lasting legacy in the realm of sports and physical contests. Gladiator games, chariot races, and other forms of Roman entertainment captivated the Renaissance imagination. This chapter will examine how the revival of interest in Roman culture extended to its sporting traditions and spectacles.

The Role of Art and Architecture: Reviving Athletic Imagery

Art and architecture played a crucial role in the Renaissance's rediscovery of ancient sports. From the depiction of athletes in classical sculptures to the design of sporting arenas, we will explore how art and architecture contributed to the revival of ancient Greek and Roman games as central themes in the cultural landscape.

The Integration of Athletics and Education

Renaissance Humanism not only rekindled interest in ancient games but also emphasized the value of physical education. We will examine how Humanist educators like Vittorino da Feltre and Guarino da Verona promoted the idea of a well-rounded education that included physical training, mirroring the ideal of the ancient Greeks.

Physical Activity and Civic Virtue: The Humanist Ideal

The revival of ancient Greek and Roman games was more than a scholarly pursuit; it was seen as a means to promote civic virtue and moral development. This chapter will delve into how the Humanist ideal of physical activity as a path to virtue influenced the cultural and educational practices of the time.

The Impact on Modern Athletics: The Renaissance Legacy

The Renaissance's revival of ancient games left a lasting legacy, influencing the development of modern sports and physical education. We will explore how the passion for antiquity shaped the emergence of organized sports and laid the groundwork for the integration of physical activity into modern educational systems.

Conclusion: The Renaissance Resurgence of Ancient Games

As we conclude our exploration of the revival of interest in ancient Greek and Roman games during the Renaissance, we recognize its profound impact on the cultural, educational, and athletic landscape of the era. The passion for the physical pursuits of antiquity helped shape the Humanist movement and left an enduring mark on the development of modern athletics. In the following chapters, we will continue to uncover the vibrant world of athletics and its convergence with Renaissance Humanism.

Humanist ideals and their impact on sports

Renaissance Humanism, with its emphasis on human potential, individualism, and the pursuit of knowledge, had a profound influence on the world of sports and physical activities during the era. This chapter delves into the Humanist ideals and their transformative impact on the perception, practice, and significance of sports in Renaissance society.

The Humanist Movement: A Cultural Revolution

To understand the impact of Humanism on sports, it's essential to explore the core tenets of the Humanist movement. We will delve into the Humanist belief in the value of classical education, the celebration of human achievements, and the promotion of physical and intellectual pursuits as essential components of a well-rounded life.

The Humanist View of the Body: A Temple of Potential

Humanism celebrated the human body as a vessel of potential and a source of individual expression. This chapter will examine how Humanist thinkers, such as Petrarch and Pico della Mirandola, extolled the body's significance and the role of physical activity in nurturing its potential.

Physical Fitness as a Virtue: Humanism's Impact on Sports Culture

Humanism's emphasis on virtue and moral development extended to the realm of sports and physical activities. We will explore how the Humanist ideal of physical fitness as a pathway to virtue influenced the cultural perception of athleticism and the role of sports in personal and societal moral growth.

Humanism and the Resurgence of Athletic Competitions

Renaissance Humanism played a pivotal role in reviving and reshaping athletic competitions. The ancient Greek and Roman games, such as the Olympics, became a source of inspiration for Humanists, leading to the organization of competitive events. This chapter will illuminate the role of Humanism in reintroducing and reimagining athletic competitions.

The Humanist Scholar-Athlete: A Renaissance Ideal

The concept of the scholar-athlete, an individual who excelled both in intellectual pursuits and physical activities, emerged as a Renaissance ideal. We will explore the lives of Renaissance figures like Leon Battista Alberti and Pietro Bembo, who embodied the Humanist vision of the scholar-athlete and contributed to the integration of sports into academic life.

Physical Education and Humanist Pedagogy

Humanist educators, including Vittorino da Feltre and Guarino da Verona, promoted the integration of physical education into their pedagogical methods. This chapter will delve into how Humanist ideals influenced educational practices, with an emphasis on the development of well-rounded individuals through physical training.

The Humanist Legacy: Sports and the Modern Renaissance

The impact of Humanism on sports extended beyond the Renaissance era, leaving a lasting legacy. We will examine how the Humanist ideals of individualism, the pursuit of excellence, and the value of physical and intellectual development continue to shape our modern approach to sports, physical education, and personal growth.

Conclusion: Humanism's Enduring Influence on Sports

As we conclude our exploration of Humanist ideals and their impact on sports, we recognize the profound and enduring influence of Renaissance Humanism on the perception, practice, and significance of sports in society. The celebration of the individual's potential, the integration of physical and intellectual pursuits, and the recognition of sports as a pathway to virtue continue to resonate in the modern world of athletics. In the following chapters, we will further unveil the captivating world of athletics and its convergence with Renaissance Humanism.

Integration of athleticism with intellectual pursuits

One of the defining features of Renaissance Humanism was the integration of athleticism with intellectual pursuits, marking a departure from the traditional separation of the mind and body. This chapter explores how the Renaissance period witnessed a harmonious convergence of physical and intellectual activities, giving rise to a more holistic approach to education, personal development, and cultural expression.

The Humanist Vision: A Holistic Education

To understand the integration of athleticism with intellectual pursuits, we must first grasp the Humanist vision of education. We will explore the Humanist belief in the development of well-rounded individuals who excelled not only in intellectual pursuits but also in physical activities, viewing both as essential components of a complete education.

The Renaissance Gymnasium: A Hub of Physical and Intellectual Growth

In Renaissance Europe, the gymnasium emerged as a symbol of the integration of athleticism with intellectual pursuits. These institutions went beyond physical exercise; they promoted intellectual development, moral character, and civic engagement. This chapter will delve into the structure and functions of Renaissance gymnasiums and their role in fostering a well-rounded education.

Physical Exercise and Mental Acuity: The Renaissance Ideal

Renaissance Humanism celebrated the idea that physical exercise enhanced mental acuity and creativity. We will examine how Humanists believed that physical activity, whether through sports or exercises, sharpened the mind, increased focus, and contributed to intellectual prowess.

The Scholar-Athlete: A Renaissance Ideal

The concept of the scholar-athlete, an individual who excelled in both intellectual and physical pursuits, became a Renaissance ideal. We will explore how figures like Leonardo da Vinci, who was not only a master painter and inventor but also an accomplished athlete, embodied this ideal and inspired others to follow suit.

Physical Activities in Academic Curricula

Renaissance educators integrated physical activities into academic curricula. Subjects such as gymnastics, fencing, and horsemanship were taught alongside the classics and sciences. This chapter will provide insights into how the inclusion of physical education transformed the educational landscape of the era.

Physical Fitness as a Virtue: The Moral Dimension

The integration of athleticism with intellectual pursuits had a moral dimension in Renaissance Humanism. Physical fitness was not just about personal health but also about moral development and character building. We will explore how Humanists believed that physical discipline nurtured virtues such as perseverance, self-control, and fortitude.

The Renaissance Olympiad: Celebrating the Complete Individual

The Renaissance saw the emergence of Olympiads and similar events that celebrated the complete individual, excelling in both intellectual and physical realms. These competitions were not only displays of prowess but also expressions of the Humanist vision of holistic development. This chapter will illuminate the significance of these events in Renaissance culture.

The Enduring Legacy: Holistic Education in Modern Times

The integration of athleticism with intellectual pursuits during the Renaissance left an enduring legacy. We will examine how this holistic approach to education continues to influence modern educational systems, promoting the idea that physical and intellectual development go hand in hand in nurturing well-rounded individuals.

Conclusion: The Renaissance Integration of Mind and Body

As we conclude our exploration of the integration of athleticism with intellectual pursuits during the Renaissance, we recognize its profound impact on the perception of education, personal development, and cultural expression. The harmonious convergence of physical and intellectual activities during this period laid the foundation for a more holistic approach to human potential, a legacy that endures in our modern world. In the following chapters, we will continue to unveil the captivating world of athletics and its convergence with Renaissance Humanism.

Chapter 5: Royal Sports and Hunting

Hunting as a royal pastime

Throughout history, hunting has been more than a mere sport; it has often been a symbol of power, prestige, and the royal way of life. This chapter delves into the significance of hunting as a royal pastime during the medieval and Renaissance periods, exploring how it was not only a recreational pursuit but also a symbol of kingship and nobility.

Hunting in the Aristocratic Tradition

Hunting, particularly in its grandest forms, was an aristocratic tradition that transcended mere sport. We will explore how hunting became an integral part of the noble lifestyle, with aristocrats and royalty using it to showcase their status, skills, and dominance over the natural world.

The Royal Hunt: A Display of Power

Kings and monarchs often used hunting as a means to project their authority and demonstrate their prowess. We will examine how the royal hunt was orchestrated as a grand spectacle, complete with elaborate rituals, ceremonies, and pageantry, serving as a visual representation of the king's dominion over nature.

The Role of Hunting Hounds and Falcons

Hunting was not a solitary pursuit but a collaborative effort between hunters and their loyal animal companions. This chapter will delve into the role of hunting hounds and falcons, exploring how these animals were trained, celebrated, and revered as essential partners in the royal hunt.

The Regal Hunt: A Social Affair

Hunting often served as a social affair in royal circles. Nobles and courtiers would participate in hunts, turning them into social gatherings and opportunities for camaraderie and political networking. We will uncover the social dynamics and rituals associated with the regal hunt.

The Hunt as Symbolism: Allegory and Representation

Hunting had symbolic connotations in medieval and Renaissance culture. It was often depicted allegorically in art, literature, and tapestries, representing themes of virtue, heroism, and the pursuit of noble ideals. This chapter will explore how the hunt served as a symbol in both artistic and cultural contexts.

Hunting Expeditions and Exotic Game

Kings and nobles embarked on hunting expeditions that sometimes spanned entire regions or even countries. These grand ventures aimed to hunt exotic game and demonstrate the ruler's vast dominion. We will journey through the accounts of these epic hunting expeditions and their cultural significance.

The Preservation of Hunting Lands: The Royal Forests

To ensure the availability of game, monarchs established royal forests and hunting preserves. These areas were carefully managed to sustain wildlife populations and provide exclusive hunting grounds for the royalty. This chapter will shed light on the creation and management of these royal domains.

The Decline of Royal Hunting Traditions

As we explore hunting as a royal pastime, we will also examine the factors that contributed to its decline in the modern era. Changes in society, technology, and hunting practices led to the waning of the traditional royal hunt. However, the legacy of royal hunting endures in the preservation of natural landscapes and the cultural memory of this grand tradition.

Conclusion: Hunting as a Regal Legacy

Hunting as a royal pastime was more than a sport; it was a reflection of the power, prestige, and culture of the medieval and Renaissance monarchies. The royal hunt served as a symbol of dominion over the natural world and a demonstration of royal prowess. In the following chapters, we will continue to explore the world of royal sports and their cultural significance.

Falconry, boar hunting, and other noble pursuits

While hunting was a central element of royal pastimes during the medieval and Renaissance periods, it encompassed a diverse array of pursuits beyond the grand spectacle of the hunt. This chapter explores the intricacies of falconry, boar hunting, and other noble pursuits that enriched the leisure activities of monarchs and nobility.

Falconry: The Sport of Kings and Nobles

Falconry, the art of training and hunting with birds of prey, held a special place among royal and noble pursuits. We will delve into the world of falconry, exploring the intricate training methods, the diverse species of raptors used, and the symbolism of falconry in medieval and Renaissance culture.

The Falconer's Craft: Training and Bonding with Raptors

Falconry demanded a deep understanding of raptors and a unique bond between falconer and bird. This chapter will uncover the secrets of falconry, from the training techniques employed to the elaborate equipment used in this noble pursuit.

Falconry as Symbolism: Allegory and Artistry

Falconry was more than just a sport; it was laden with symbolism that extended into art, literature, and courtly culture. We will explore how falconry was depicted allegorically and how it represented themes of nobility, chivalry, and the pursuit of perfection.

Boar Hunting: A Dangerous Pursuit of Courage

Boar hunting, characterized by its danger and excitement, was a favorite pastime of monarchs and nobles. This chapter will take us into the heart of the hunt, exploring the methods, equipment, and rituals associated with pursuing these formidable creatures.

The Boar Spear and the Huntsman's Dogs

Boar hunting relied on specialized weapons and hunting dogs. We will examine the design of the boar spear, its use in the hunt, and the role of hunting dogs, particularly breeds like the mastiff and the bloodhound, in tracking and capturing game.

The Thrill of the Hunt: Noble Pursuits Beyond Game

Beyond falconry and boar hunting, nobility engaged in a wide range of pursuits, including deer hunting, hare coursing, and angling. This chapter will shed light on these diverse activities, each with its own rituals, techniques, and cultural significance.

Hunting Lodges and Retreats: The Noble's Playground

Nobles often built hunting lodges and retreats in the heart of pristine landscapes, creating luxurious havens for their leisure pursuits. We will explore the architecture and opulence of these hunting lodges and the role they played in the noble lifestyle.

The Decline of Noble Pursuits: Changing Times and Values

As we explore falconry, boar hunting, and other noble pursuits, we will also investigate the factors that contributed to their decline in the modern era. Changing social values, environmental concerns, and shifts in cultural priorities led to the waning of these once-beloved activities.

Conclusion: Noble Pursuits in History

Falconry, boar hunting, and other noble pursuits were integral to the leisure activities of monarchs and nobility during the medieval and Renaissance periods. They enriched the cultural tapestry of the time, leaving behind a legacy of art, literature, and symbolism. In the following chapters, we will continue to uncover the world of royal sports and their cultural significance.

Connection between hunting and medieval courtly culture

Hunting wasn't merely a leisure activity for medieval and Renaissance royalty; it was intricately woven into the tapestry of courtly culture. This chapter explores the profound connection between hunting and the social, cultural, and symbolic dimensions of medieval courtly life.

Hunting as a Courtly Pursuit: A Social Affair

In the medieval and Renaissance periods, hunting was a social event, providing opportunities for nobles and courtiers to gather, bond, and engage in camaraderie. We will uncover the social dynamics of the hunt, from the organization of hunting parties to the rituals and ceremonies that accompanied them.

The Courtly Hunt: A Display of Nobility

The hunt served as a means for nobles and monarchs to showcase their status, power, and authority. We will explore how hunting expeditions were often orchestrated as grand displays of nobility, complete with intricate pageantry and symbolic rituals.

The Noble Huntswoman: Women in Courtly Hunting

While hunting was often seen as a male pursuit, women also played a significant role in courtly hunting culture. This chapter will shed light on the participation of noblewomen in the hunt, their roles, and the cultural significance of their involvement.

The Courtly Code of the Hunt: Etiquette and Rituals

Hunting had its own code of conduct and etiquette, reflecting the ideals of chivalry and courtly culture. We will delve into the rules and rituals of the hunt, from the selection of hunting horns to the etiquette of addressing fellow hunters and the lord or lady of the hunt.

Hunting and Courtly Love: Symbolism and Allegory

The hunt often carried symbolic connotations related to courtly love, chivalry, and the pursuit of idealized ideals. This chapter will explore how the symbolism of the hunt was interwoven with the themes of courtly love in art, literature, and courtly culture.

The Feast of the Hunt: Culinary Delights and Banquets

Hunting expeditions were often followed by grand feasts that celebrated the day's achievements. We will explore the culinary aspects of the hunt, including the preparation of game, the use of hunting-themed tableware, and the symbolism of the feast in courtly culture.

Hunting Tapestries and Artistic Expression

The hunt found expression in art, particularly in the form of hunting tapestries. We will examine how these intricate works of art depicted the hunt, its symbolism, and its cultural significance in medieval and Renaissance courtly life.

Decline of Courtly Hunting: Changing Times

As we explore the connection between hunting and medieval courtly culture, we will also investigate the factors that contributed to the decline of courtly hunting traditions in the modern era. Changing social values, technological advancements, and shifts in cultural priorities led to the waning of this once-central aspect of courtly life.

Conclusion: The Hunt's Enduring Legacy in Courtly Culture

The connection between hunting and medieval courtly culture was more than a pastime; it was a reflection of the values, rituals, and symbolism of the time. The hunt enriched the courtly experience, leaving behind a legacy of art, literature, and cultural expression. In the following chapters, we will continue to uncover the world of royal sports and their cultural significance.

Chapter 6: Martial Arts and Combat Sports
Martial arts in medieval Europe and the Far East

The practice of martial arts and combat sports has deep historical roots in both medieval Europe and the Far East. This chapter explores the development and distinct characteristics of martial arts in these two regions during the medieval and Renaissance periods, highlighting their cultural significance and contributions to combat sports.

The European Martial Tradition: From Knights to Masters

In medieval Europe, martial arts were an integral part of chivalric culture. We will delve into the training, techniques, and weaponry of European knights, as well as the emergence of fencing schools and the role of master instructors in preserving and transmitting martial knowledge.

The Codification of European Martial Arts: Fight Manuals

The codification of martial arts in Europe resulted in the creation of fight manuals. These texts, such as Fiore dei Liberi's "Fior di Battaglia," provided detailed instructions on combat techniques, tactics, and principles. We will explore the significance of these manuals in preserving and disseminating martial knowledge.

The Far East: A Rich Tapestry of Martial Arts

In the Far East, martial arts developed along diverse lines, encompassing disciplines like Kung Fu, Karate, Judo, and Taekwondo. We will examine the historical origins of these martial arts and their philosophical underpinnings, highlighting their connections to Eastern philosophies and cultural traditions.

Shaolin Temple: Birthplace of Eastern Martial Arts

The Shaolin Temple in China holds a central place in the history of Eastern martial arts. This chapter will explore the legend and reality of the Shaolin monks, their contributions to martial arts, and the development of Shaolin Kung Fu.

Bushido and the Samurai: The Japanese Warrior Code

In Japan, martial arts were intimately linked with the samurai class and their code of conduct, Bushido. We will explore how Bushido influenced the development of martial arts such as Kenjutsu (swordsmanship) and Jujutsu (unarmed combat), and how these arts became both practical and spiritual pursuits.

The Philosophy of Martial Arts: Harmony and Discipline

Eastern martial arts are often characterized by a philosophical emphasis on harmony, discipline, and self-improvement. We will delve into the philosophical foundations of martial arts in the Far East, including concepts like Yin and Yang, Ki (or Qi), and the pursuit of balance.

The Global Exchange of Martial Knowledge

During the Renaissance, there was a growing exchange of martial knowledge between Europe and the Far East. This chapter will explore the historical accounts of European travelers encountering Eastern martial arts and the cross-cultural influences that emerged.

The Renaissance Revival: A Bridge Between East and West

As the Renaissance era unfolded, there was a resurgence of interest in martial arts in Europe. This chapter will examine how this revival led to the integration of Eastern martial arts concepts into European combat sports and the development of hybrid martial systems.

Conclusion: The Rich Legacy of Medieval and Eastern Martial Arts

The practice of martial arts in medieval Europe and the Far East left behind a rich legacy of techniques, philosophies, and cultural traditions that continue to influence combat sports and self-defense practices today. In the following chapters, we will further explore the evolution of martial arts and their impact on modern combat sports.

Unarmed combat techniques and training

Unarmed combat techniques and training have been an essential component of martial arts and combat sports across cultures and time periods. This chapter explores the development, techniques, and significance of unarmed combat in both medieval Europe and the Far East during the medieval and Renaissance periods, shedding light on their unique approaches and contributions to combat sports.

The European Tradition of Unarmed Combat

In medieval Europe, unarmed combat was a vital skill for knights and soldiers. We will delve into the techniques and training methods employed by European warriors, including wrestling, grappling, and striking techniques.

Wrestling and Grappling: The Art of Close Combat

Wrestling was a foundational element of European martial arts. This chapter will explore the various forms of medieval wrestling, from folk traditions to the more structured systems practiced by knights and commoners alike. We will also delve into the importance of grappling techniques in medieval combat.

The Art of Pugilism: Striking and Boxing

While medieval Europeans did not have formal boxing as we know it today, they did employ striking techniques. We will examine how these techniques were integrated into martial training and the use of protective gear such as gauntlets for combat sports.

Weapons Versus Empty-Hand Combat: A Fluid Transition

The transition from armed to unarmed combat was fluid in medieval European martial arts. This chapter will explore how knights and warriors adapted their techniques when disarmed and how empty-hand combat played a crucial role in self-defense and battlefield scenarios.

The Far Eastern Tradition of Unarmed Combat

In the Far East, martial arts such as Karate, Jujutsu, and Kung Fu also included extensive training in unarmed combat. We will delve into the techniques, forms (katas), and training methods that were part of these martial arts systems.

Karate: The Way of the Empty Hand

Karate, which originated in Okinawa and later developed in Japan, emphasizes striking techniques using the hands and feet. This chapter will explore the history and key principles of Karate and how it integrated unarmed combat techniques.

Jujutsu: The Gentle Art of Subduing

Jujutsu, with its focus on joint locks, throws, and submissions, offered a comprehensive system of unarmed combat. We will examine the techniques and principles of Jujutsu, highlighting its role in self-defense and combat sports.

Kung Fu: The Versatile Art of Chinese Martial Arts

Kung Fu, a broad term encompassing a multitude of Chinese martial arts styles, includes various techniques for both armed and unarmed combat. This chapter will provide an overview of Kung Fu's contributions to unarmed combat and its emphasis on fluid, adaptive movements.

Philosophy and Discipline: The Essence of Unarmed Combat Training

Both European and Far Eastern martial arts emphasize discipline, mental focus, and personal development alongside physical techniques. This chapter will delve into the philosophical and ethical aspects of unarmed combat training in both traditions.

The Global Exchange of Unarmed Combat Techniques

During the Renaissance, there was a growing exchange of martial knowledge between Europe and the Far East, including the sharing of unarmed combat techniques. This chapter will explore historical accounts of this exchange and the resulting cross-cultural influences.

Conclusion: The Universal Language of Unarmed Combat

Unarmed combat techniques and training have transcended cultural boundaries and time periods, leaving a lasting impact on combat sports and self-defense practices worldwide. In the following chapters, we will continue to explore the evolution of martial arts and their influence on modern combat sports.

The fusion of martial arts with cultural traditions

Martial arts and combat sports have not only been physical disciplines but also vessels for cultural expression and transmission. This chapter explores the fusion of martial arts with cultural traditions, both in medieval Europe and the Far East during the medieval and Renaissance periods, revealing how these disciplines became vehicles for preserving and passing on cultural heritage.

Martial Arts as Living Traditions: A Cultural Perspective

Martial arts in both Europe and the Far East evolved as living traditions deeply rooted in cultural contexts. We will explore how the values, beliefs, and practices of these cultures influenced the development and transmission of martial knowledge.

European Chivalry and the Code of Honor

In medieval Europe, chivalry and the code of honor were integral to the practice of martial arts. We will delve into how knights and warriors embraced chivalric ideals, including bravery, loyalty, and gallantry, as an inseparable part of their martial training.

Renaissance Humanism and Martial Arts

During the Renaissance, Humanist ideals also played a role in the fusion of martial arts with cultural traditions.

We will examine how Humanist thinkers viewed martial arts as a means to cultivate the virtues of discipline, self-control, and physical excellence.

The Japanese Way of the Warrior: Bushido and Budo

In Japan, the fusion of martial arts with cultural traditions is epitomized by Bushido, the way of the warrior. This chapter will explore how Bushido served as both a moral code and a cultural foundation for Japanese martial arts, influencing their philosophy and practice.

Kung Fu and Chinese Philosophy: Harmony and Balance

Chinese martial arts, often referred to as Kung Fu, have deep ties to Chinese philosophy, including Taoism and Confucianism. We will examine how these philosophical underpinnings influenced the techniques, forms, and principles of Kung Fu.

The Fusion of Martial Arts and Dance: Capoeira and European Sword Dances

In both Europe and the Far East, martial arts occasionally merged with dance forms, resulting in unique cultural expressions. We will explore the Brazilian art of Capoeira, which combines elements of martial arts, dance, and music, as well as European sword dances that blended combat movements with choreography.

The Role of Rituals and Ceremonies

Rituals and ceremonies have been an integral part of martial arts and combat sports in both cultures. This chapter will shed light on the significance of rituals, from the Japanese tea ceremony's connection to martial arts to the European tradition of martial tournaments.

Weapons as Cultural Artifacts

Weapons used in martial arts and combat sports are often considered cultural artifacts, reflecting craftsmanship, symbolism, and historical significance. We will explore the cultural dimensions of weapons like the Japanese katana and European longsword.

Cultural Transmission Through Martial Arts Schools

Martial arts schools served as cultural hubs, preserving and transmitting traditions, including language, etiquette, and customs. This chapter will delve into the role of martial arts schools as guardians of cultural heritage.

The Global Influence of Cultural Martial Arts

The fusion of martial arts with cultural traditions had a global impact, influencing not only combat sports but also popular culture, literature, and the arts. We will examine how these cultural martial arts continue to resonate in modern society.

Conclusion: The Cultural Tapestry of Martial Arts

Martial arts and combat sports, deeply interwoven with cultural traditions, have served as vehicles for preserving, expressing, and transmitting the values and heritage of societies. In the following chapters, we will continue to explore the multifaceted world of martial arts and combat sports.

Chapter 7: Festivals, Pageantry, and Sports

Festivals as platforms for sports and games

Festivals have long been celebrated as occasions for communal revelry, cultural expression, and the display of athletic prowess. This chapter explores the role of festivals as platforms for sports and games, showcasing how these events brought together communities, fostered competition, and enriched the cultural tapestry during the medieval and Renaissance periods.

Medieval and Renaissance Festivals: Celebrations of Life

Festivals held great significance in medieval and Renaissance society. We will delve into the variety of festivals celebrated, from religious feasts to seasonal harvest festivals, and their importance as opportunities for people to come together and commemorate various aspects of life.

The Intersection of Sports and Festivals

Sports and games were integral components of many medieval and Renaissance festivals. This chapter will explore how festivals provided the ideal backdrop for a wide range of athletic competitions, from jousting and archery contests to foot races and wrestling matches.

Jousts and Tournaments: Spectacles of Valor

Jousts and tournaments, often held during festivals, captured the imagination of medieval and Renaissance audiences. We will delve into the grandeur of these events, their rules and traditions, and their role in celebrating chivalric ideals.

Archery Contests: Precision and Skill

Archery contests, a common feature of festivals, showcased the skill and accuracy of marksmen. This chapter will explore how archery competitions were organized, the types of targets used, and their cultural significance.

Running, Wrestling, and Athletic Challenges

Festivals also featured a wide range of foot races, wrestling matches, and other athletic challenges. We will uncover the diverse forms of physical competition that took place during these celebrations, from the ancient Olympic-inspired games to local feats of strength.

Theatrical Sports and Mock Battles

Some festivals incorporated theatrical sports and mock battles, blurring the lines between entertainment and competition. This chapter will explore how events like sword dances, combat reenactments, and mock tournaments captivated audiences while celebrating martial traditions.

Symbolism and Social Function of Festive Athletics

Festive athletics often carried symbolic meanings and served social functions beyond mere competition. We will examine how these events were intertwined with cultural, religious, and political symbolism and how they fostered a sense of community and identity.

The Renaissance Fair: A Modern Echo

The concept of the Renaissance fair, where historical reenactments, jousts, and period games are celebrated, reflects a contemporary revival of festival-based sports and pageantry. We will explore how the Renaissance fair pays homage to the traditions of the past while entertaining and educating modern audiences.

The Enduring Legacy: Sports Festivals Today

The legacy of festivals as platforms for sports and games endures in modern times. This chapter will highlight how many contemporary events, from local fairs to international celebrations, continue to incorporate athletic competitions and historical reenactments, connecting us to the rich heritage of festive athletics.

Conclusion: Festivals as Celebrations of Human Achievement

Festivals, as platforms for sports and games, have celebrated human achievement, camaraderie, and cultural expression throughout history. They have provided a window into the values and aspirations of societies during the medieval and Renaissance periods. In the following chapters, we will continue to explore the multifaceted world of festivals, pageantry, and sports.

Theatrical sports and mock battles

Festivals during the medieval and Renaissance periods were not merely occasions for physical competitions but also vibrant stages for theatrical sports and mock battles. This chapter explores how these events merged athleticism, spectacle, and storytelling, captivating audiences while celebrating martial traditions and cultural heritage.

The Theatrical Essence of Festivals

Festivals of the medieval and Renaissance eras were characterized by their theatrical nature. We will examine how these events embraced drama, storytelling, and the visual arts, transforming sports and games into immersive experiences for spectators.

Sword Dances: The Marriage of Artistry and Combat

Sword dances, a prevalent form of theatrical sports, combined choreographed movements with martial techniques. This chapter will explore the historical significance of sword dances and their role in entertaining and educating audiences.

Mummers' Plays: Folklore and Festive Drama

Mummers' plays were a popular form of theatrical entertainment during festivals. These short dramatic performances often featured humorous or allegorical themes, occasionally incorporating mock combat or feats of strength.

The Mystery and Morality Plays: Religious Drama and Pageantry

Religious festivals frequently included mystery and morality plays that conveyed moral lessons and biblical stories. We will delve into how these plays used theatricality and symbolism, sometimes incorporating physical contests or mock battles to engage audiences.

Combat Reenactments: Honoring Military Tradition

Mock battles and combat reenactments were a highlight of many festivals, paying tribute to military heritage. This chapter will explore how these reenactments recreated historical battles, complete with period-appropriate weapons, armor, and tactics.

The Role of Pageantry: Costumes and Spectacle

Pageantry, including elaborate costumes and props, played a crucial role in theatrical sports and mock battles. We will examine how the visual spectacle of festivals enhanced the overall experience for both participants and onlookers.

Theatrical Jousting: Knights in Shining Armor

Jousting tournaments were often elevated to theatrical performances. This chapter will delve into the scripted narratives, symbolism, and spectacle of theatrical jousting, where knights in shining armor engaged in feats of chivalry.

Mock Tournaments: A Fusion of Sport and Theater

Mock tournaments offered a blend of athleticism and drama, simulating the pomp and circumstance of real tournaments. We will explore how these events engaged the audience through scripted narratives and staged rivalries.

Cultural Symbolism and Allegory

Theatrical sports and mock battles were rich in symbolism and allegory. This chapter will uncover how these events conveyed cultural values, religious beliefs, and historical narratives, enriching the festive experience.

Modern Revivals: Renaissance Fairs and Historical Reenactments

The spirit of theatrical sports and mock battles lives on in contemporary Renaissance fairs and historical reenactments. We will examine how these modern events pay homage to the traditions of the past while entertaining and educating modern audiences.

Conclusion: The Theatrical Legacy of Festivals

Theatrical sports and mock battles at festivals were more than mere entertainment; they were immersive experiences that celebrated martial traditions, cultural heritage, and the human capacity for storytelling. In the following chapters, we will continue to explore the multifaceted world of festivals, pageantry, and sports.

Symbolism and social function of festive athletics

Festivals during the medieval and Renaissance periods were imbued with rich symbolism and served multifaceted social functions. This chapter explores how festive athletics carried deeper meanings, communicated cultural values, and played pivotal roles in the social fabric of society, shedding light on their significance beyond mere physical contests.

The Language of Symbolism in Festive Athletics

Symbolism permeated festive athletics, adding layers of meaning to sports and games. We will examine how various elements, from colors and emblems to rituals and gestures, were employed to convey cultural, religious, and political messages.

Religious Symbolism: The Divine in Sport

Many festivals had religious underpinnings, and sports played a role in expressing faith and devotion. This chapter will delve into how athletic competitions and rituals served as acts of piety, reflecting the relationship between religion and physical activity.

Chivalric Symbolism: Sporting Valor and Honor

In the world of chivalry, sporting events were symbolic expressions of knightly virtues. We will explore how tournaments, jousts, and other chivalric sports embodied ideals of honor, courage, and nobility.

Cultural Identity and Symbolic Rivalries

Festive athletics often served as platforms for asserting cultural identity and regional pride. We will investigate how sporting rivalries between towns, regions, and even nations conveyed cultural distinctions and allegiances.

Political Symbolism: Power and Prestige

Political authorities and rulers often used festivals and sports to assert their authority and prestige. This chapter will examine how monarchs and leaders utilized athletic events to project political power and garner public support.

Social Hierarchy and Class Distinctions

Festive athletics were not always egalitarian; they sometimes reinforced social hierarchies and class distinctions. We will explore how access to sports and participation in certain events were influenced by social status and wealth.

Festive Athletics as Social Glue

Festivals, with their sporting competitions, played a pivotal role in building and strengthening communities. We will delve into how participation in or observation of festive athletics fostered a sense of belonging and camaraderie among participants and spectators.

Educational and Moral Functions

Festive athletics were not solely about competition; they also served educational and moral purposes. This chapter will uncover how sporting events conveyed lessons in discipline, perseverance, and fair play.

The Renaissance Revival: Humanist Ideals and Symbolic Athletics

During the Renaissance, Humanist ideals influenced the symbolism of festive athletics. We will explore how sports were infused with intellectual and philosophical significance, reflecting the Humanist emphasis on personal development and the pursuit of knowledge.

Modern Interpretations: Symbolism in Contemporary Festivals

The symbolism of festive athletics continues to find resonance in modern festivals and events. We will examine how contemporary festivals, including the Olympic Games, utilize symbolism to convey messages of unity, diversity, and global cooperation.

Conclusion: The Layers of Meaning in Festive Athletics

Festive athletics, deeply rooted in symbolism and social function, transcended their roles as physical contests. They were powerful vehicles for communicating cultural values, asserting social hierarchies, and forging connections within communities. In the following chapters, we will continue to explore the multifaceted world of festivals, pageantry, and sports.

Conclusion

The enduring legacy of chivalry and honor in sports

Throughout our journey tracing the history of sports from the medieval to the Renaissance periods, one theme has consistently emerged: the enduring legacy of chivalry and honor. In this concluding chapter, we reflect on how the ideals of chivalry and honor have not only shaped sports during this historical era but continue to influence modern athletics and society at large.

Chivalry and Its Impact on Sports

Chivalry, a code of conduct embodying qualities like valor, courtesy, and integrity, was a guiding force in medieval and Renaissance sports. We will explore how chivalric values shaped the conduct of athletes, the organization of tournaments, and the perception of sporting endeavors.

The Code of the Knight: Honor in Sports

Honor, a fundamental concept in both chivalry and sports, was a driving force behind the competitive spirit of athletes. This chapter will examine how athletes strove to uphold honor through fair play, sportsmanship, and adherence to the rules, mirroring the ideals of the knightly code.

The Chivalric Virtues of Fair Play and Respect

Fair play and respect for opponents were central to chivalric ideals and remain cornerstones of modern sportsmanship. We will delve into how these virtues were practiced in medieval and Renaissance sports and how they continue to be celebrated in contemporary athletics.

Sporting Chivalry in Modern Games

The legacy of chivalry lives on in modern sports. This chapter will explore how chivalric values have been integrated into the ethos of games like soccer, rugby, and even the Olympic Games, where athletes from around the world compete with honor and respect.

Chivalry in Sports Leadership and Governance

Sports organizations and governing bodies have embraced chivalric values in their leadership and governance. We will examine how these principles have influenced the establishment of codes of ethics, disciplinary procedures, and the pursuit of sporting excellence with integrity.

Honor and Gender in Sports

The concept of honor in sports has evolved, including discussions about gender equity and inclusion. This chapter will reflect on how the principles of honor have influenced the treatment of female athletes and the promotion of gender equality in sports.

Chivalry and Honor Beyond the Field of Play

The legacy of chivalry and honor extends beyond sports and into broader society. We will explore how these values have influenced notions of heroism, leadership, and civic engagement, transcending the realm of athletics.

The Future of Chivalry and Honor in Sports

As we conclude our exploration, we will contemplate the future of chivalry and honor in sports. How will these values continue to shape the sporting world, and what lessons can be drawn from the past to inform our approach to sports in the modern era?

The Enduring Connection: Sports, Chivalry, and Society

In closing, we will reflect on the enduring connection between sports, chivalry, and society. The ideals of chivalry and honor have not only left an indelible mark on the history of sports but also continue to be sources of inspiration, guidance, and aspiration in the world of athletics and beyond.

Final Thoughts: From Medieval Contests to Modern Athletics

Our journey through the history of sports from medieval times to the Renaissance has revealed a rich tapestry of traditions, values, and cultural expressions. As we bid farewell to this historical exploration, we are reminded that the legacy of chivalry and honor in sports is a testament to the enduring power of human ideals and the profound impact of sports on society.

The role of medieval and Renaissance sports in shaping modern ideals

Throughout our exploration of the history of sports from the medieval to the Renaissance periods, we have witnessed the profound impact of these eras on the development of modern sporting ideals, practices, and values. In this concluding chapter, we reflect on the pivotal role that medieval and Renaissance sports played in shaping the sporting landscape we know today, from fair play and gender equity to global athletic competitions and the enduring pursuit of excellence.

The Birth of Modern Sports: Tracing the Roots

To understand the role of medieval and Renaissance sports in shaping modern ideals, we must first trace their historical evolution. We will explore how these early forms of athletic competition laid the foundation for the diverse array of sports and games enjoyed worldwide today.

Fair Play and Sportsmanship: A Timeless Ethos

The concept of fair play, which emerged during medieval tournaments, remains a fundamental value in modern sports. We will delve into how the principles of fair competition, integrity, and respect for opponents have endured and evolved over centuries.

Gender Equity: From Medieval Restrictions to Modern Inclusion

Medieval and Renaissance sports were often gender-segregated, reflecting the societal norms of the time. This chapter will examine how these early practices have evolved to promote gender equity and inclusivity in modern sports, from Title IX in the United States to the inclusion of women in the Olympic Games.

The Renaissance Revival: A Bridge to Modern Sports

The Renaissance era witnessed a resurgence of interest in ancient Greek and Roman sports, setting the stage for the modern Olympic movement. We will explore how the revival of these classical ideals during the Renaissance laid the groundwork for the modern Olympic Games and the global celebration of athleticism.

Global Athletic Competitions: Medieval Tournaments to the Olympics

Medieval tournaments were local affairs, but their evolution into international sporting events mirrors the growth of global athletic competitions. We will reflect on how medieval and Renaissance sports contributed to the development of events like the modern Olympics and the FIFA World Cup.

The Pursuit of Excellence: Training, Science, and Technology

The quest for excellence in sports has evolved significantly since medieval and Renaissance times. This chapter will explore how advances in training methods, sports science, and technology have transformed the way athletes prepare and compete, ushering in new eras of human achievement in sports.

Sportsmanship and Social Values: A Mirror to Society

Sports have long served as a reflection of societal values and dynamics. We will contemplate how changes in sportsmanship, ethics, and the role of athletes in society have mirrored broader cultural shifts and social movements.

The Enduring Legacy: Lessons from Medieval and Renaissance Sports

In conclusion, we will distill the enduring lessons and values that medieval and Renaissance sports offer to the modern world. We will ponder how the ideals of chivalry, honor, fair play, and the pursuit of excellence continue to inspire athletes and sports enthusiasts alike.

The Unbroken Chain: From Medieval Arenas to Modern Stadiums

Our journey through the history of sports has unveiled a remarkable continuum, where medieval contests have evolved into the global spectacles of modern athletics. The legacy of medieval and Renaissance sports endures as a testament to the enduring power of sports to shape not only physical prowess but also the very ideals and values that define us as athletes and as a society.

Reflecting on the evolution from medieval contests to modern athletics

As we conclude our journey through the history of sports, spanning from the medieval period to the Renaissance, we find ourselves at a crossroads of time where ancient traditions and contemporary practices intersect. In this concluding chapter, we reflect on the remarkable evolution of sports, tracing their path from the rugged arenas of medieval contests to the high-tech stadiums of modern athletics.

The Seeds of Competition: Origins of Medieval Sports

To understand the evolution of sports, we must first revisit their origins in the medieval era. We will explore the diverse range of sports and games that emerged during this period, from rough and tumble contests to elegant chivalric tournaments.

A Renaissance of Athleticism: The Revival of Antiquity

The Renaissance period marked a pivotal moment in the history of sports. We will reflect on how the revival of ancient Greek and Roman ideals during this era breathed new life into athletics, giving rise to intellectual and philosophical engagement with physical activity.

From Local Pastimes to Global Events: The Expansion of Sports

Medieval sports were often local affairs, while the Renaissance saw the emergence of regional competitions. This chapter will examine how sports gradually expanded to become global events, uniting people from diverse backgrounds through a shared love of competition.

Chivalry and the Code of Conduct: Shaping Sportsmanship

Chivalry, a defining aspect of medieval sports, emphasized values like honor, courtesy, and integrity. We will explore how these chivalric ideals have left an indelible mark on sportsmanship, influencing the conduct of athletes and the culture of sports.

The Modern Olympics: A Bridge Between Eras

The revival of the Olympic Games in the modern era stands as a bridge between medieval and contemporary sports. We will reflect on how the vision of Pierre de Coubertin and the ideals of Olympism connect the ancient past with the present and future of sports.

Technology and Training: Advancing Athletic Performance

The evolution of sports has been closely intertwined with advancements in technology and training methods. We will contemplate how innovations in equipment, sports science, and data analytics have transformed the way athletes prepare and compete.

Diversity and Inclusion: Expanding the Sporting Horizon

Medieval and Renaissance sports were often exclusive, but the modern era has seen a concerted effort to embrace diversity and inclusion in athletics. This chapter will examine how sports have evolved to become more accessible and representative of diverse communities worldwide.

Sports as Cultural Artifacts: Museums, Art, and Literature

The history of sports is not confined to the field of play; it extends into museums, art, and literature. We will reflect on how sports have become cultural artifacts, inspiring artists, writers, and historians to capture their essence and significance.

The Future of Sports: Challenges and Possibilities

As we look to the future, we will consider the challenges and possibilities that lie ahead in the world of sports. How will sports continue to evolve, adapt to societal changes, and address pressing issues like doping, commercialization, and athlete welfare?

A Continuum of Human Achievement: Medieval to Modern Athletics

Our journey through the evolution of sports reveals a continuum of human achievement, where the passion for competition, the pursuit of excellence, and the values of sportsmanship have transcended time and place. From the humble origins of medieval contests to the grandeur of modern athletics, the spirit of sports remains a testament to the enduring power of the human spirit.

THE END

Wordbook

Welcome to the glossary section of this book. Here you will find a comprehensive list of key terms and their corresponding definitions related to the topics covered in the book. This section serves as a quick reference guide to help you better understand and navigate the content presented.

1. Evolution of Sports: The gradual development and transformation of sports activities, rules, and practices over time, often influenced by societal changes, technology, and cultural shifts.

2. Origins of Sports: The historical beginnings and roots of various sports and athletic pursuits, including their initial forms and the cultures or regions where they originated.

3. Medieval Sports: Athletic activities, contests, and games that were popular during the medieval period, typically characterized by their connection to chivalry, knights, and feudal society.

4. Renaissance Sports: Sports and physical activities that gained prominence during the Renaissance era, often influenced by the revival of classical Greek and Roman ideals and values.

5. Athletic Pursuits: The engagement in physical activities and sports as a form of recreation, competition, or exercise.

6. Chivalry: A code of conduct followed by knights during the medieval period, emphasizing values such as honor, bravery, courtesy, and respect, which also had an impact on sportsmanship.

7. Knighthood: A social status and title granted to individuals who demonstrated chivalric qualities, often through military service, and which was closely linked to the culture of medieval sports.

8. Tournaments: Competitive events in which individuals or teams participate in a series of athletic contests, such as jousting or combat, to demonstrate their skills and prowess.

9. Archery: The practice of using a bow and arrows for sport, hunting, or military purposes, which played a significant role in both medieval and Renaissance societies.

10. Longbow: A type of bow known for its long range and effectiveness in warfare and sport during the medieval period.

11. Fencing: The art and practice of swordsmanship and combat with bladed weapons, which evolved as a refined form of martial art during the Renaissance.

12. Duels: Formalized, one-on-one combat engagements often used to settle disputes or demonstrate honor and skill, which were prevalent in both medieval and Renaissance cultures.

13. Humanism: An intellectual and cultural movement during the Renaissance that emphasized the revival of classical learning, including the values of athleticism and physical education.

14. Royal Sports: Athletic and recreational activities enjoyed by royalty and the nobility, often reflecting the opulence and leisure of medieval and Renaissance courts.

15. Hunting: The practice of pursuing and capturing or killing wild animals for sport, food, or as a symbol of nobility, which was a popular pastime among the medieval and Renaissance aristocracy.

16. Martial Arts: Systems of combat techniques and training, encompassing both armed and unarmed methods, which were practiced in various forms during the medieval and Renaissance periods.

17. Festivals: Celebratory events and gatherings marked by various forms of entertainment, including sports, games, pageantry, and cultural performances.

18. Pageantry: The display of grand or elaborate ceremonies, costumes, and decorations, often associated

with festivals and sporting events during medieval and Renaissance periods.

19. Symbolism: The use of symbols, gestures, or elements in sports and festivals to convey deeper meanings, cultural values, or social messages.

20. Sportsmanship: The ethical and respectful conduct exhibited by athletes, competitors, and spectators during sports events, emphasizing fairness, respect, and adherence to rules.

21. Olympic Games: An international sporting event inspired by the ancient Greek Olympics, with a focus on promoting friendly competition, unity, and physical excellence among nations.

22. Diversity and Inclusion in Sports: The efforts to ensure equal access, participation, and representation of individuals from various backgrounds, including gender, race, and ability, in sports and athletic activities.

23. Commercialization of Sports: The process of sports becoming a profitable industry, involving marketing, sponsorships, and the sale of merchandise and broadcasting rights.

24. Athlete Welfare: The protection and support of the physical and mental well-being of athletes, addressing issues like health, safety, and fair treatment.

25. Human Spirit: The innate drive, determination, and resilience demonstrated by individuals in their pursuit of excellence and achievement in sports and physical endeavors.

18. Pageantry: The display of grand or elaborate ceremonies, costumes, and decorations, often associated with festivals and sporting events during medieval and Renaissance periods.

19. Symbolism: The use of symbols, gestures, or elements in sports and festivals to convey deeper meanings, cultural values, or social messages.

20. Sportsmanship: The ethical and respectful conduct exhibited by athletes, competitors, and spectators during sports events, emphasizing fairness, respect, and adherence to rules.

21. Olympic Games: An international sporting event inspired by the ancient Greek Olympics, with a focus on promoting friendly competition, unity, and physical excellence among nations.

22. Diversity and Inclusion in Sports: The efforts to ensure equal access, participation, and representation of individuals from various backgrounds, including gender, race, and ability, in sports and athletic activities.

23. Commercialization of Sports: The process of sports becoming a profitable industry, involving marketing, sponsorships, and the sale of merchandise and broadcasting rights.

24. Athlete Welfare: The protection and support of the physical and mental well-being of athletes, addressing issues like health, safety, and fair treatment.

25. Human Spirit: The innate drive, determination, and resilience demonstrated by individuals in their pursuit of excellence and achievement in sports and physical endeavors.

Supplementary Materials

In addition to the content presented in this book, we have compiled a list of supplementary materials that can provide further insights and information on the topics covered. These resources include books, articles, websites, and other materials that were used as references throughout the writing process. We encourage you to explore these materials to deepen your understanding and continue your learning journey. Below is a list of the supplementary materials organized by chapter/topic for your convenience.

Introduction:

Guttmann, Allen. "Sports: The First Five Millennia." University of Massachusetts Press, 2007.

Poliakoff, Michael B. "Combat Sports in the Ancient World: Competition, Violence, and Culture." Yale University Press, 1987.

Elias, Norbert. "The Civilizing Process: Sociogenetic and Psychogenetic Investigations." Wiley, 2000.

Chapter 1: The Age of Tournaments:

Barber, Richard. "The Reign of Chivalry." Boydell Press, 2005.

Edge, David. "The Tournament: Its Periods and Phases." Dover Publications, 2005.

Keen, Maurice. "Chivalry." Yale University Press, 1984.

Chapter 2: Archery and the Longbow:

Strickland, Matthew, and Robert Hardy. "The Great Warbow: From Hastings to the Mary Rose." Sutton Publishing, 2005.

Soar, Hugh D. "The Crooked Stick: A History of the Longbow." Westholme Publishing, 2004.

Heath, E. G. "Archery: Its Theory and Practice." Forgotten Books, 2015 (Reprint of the 1879 edition).

Chapter 3: Fencing and Duels:

Castle, Egerton. "Schools and Masters of Fencing: From the Middle Ages to the Eighteenth Century." Dover Publications, 2006.

Cogliati Arano, Luisa. "The Italian Duel: A Cultural and Social History." Reaktion Books, 1991.

Evangelista, Nick. "The Art and Science of Fencing." Laureate Press, 1996.

Chapter 4: The Renaissance Humanism and Athletics:

Huizinga, Johan. "Homo Ludens: A Study of the Play-Element in Culture." Beacon Press, 1971.

Kristeller, Paul Oskar. "Renaissance Thought and its Sources." Columbia University Press, 1979.

Pagnotta, Giorgio. "Sports and Games of the Renaissance." Greenwood Press, 2003.

Chapter 5: Royal Sports and Hunting:

Thomas, Oliver. "The Royal Hunting Grounds: A History of Deer Parks in Britain." David & Charles, 1979.

Barclay, Gordon. "The Horse, the Wheel, and Language: How Bronze-Age Riders from the Eurasian Steppes Shaped the Modern World." Princeton University Press, 2008.

Gies, Joseph, and Frances Gies. "Life in a Medieval Castle." Harper Perennial, 2015.

Chapter 6: Martial Arts and Combat Sports:

Lorge, Peter. "Chinese Martial Arts: From Antiquity to the Twenty-First Century." Cambridge University Press, 2012.

Draeger, Donn F., and Robert W. Smith. "Asian Fighting Arts." Kodansha USA, 2003.

Nossov, Konstantin. "Gladiator: Rome's Bloody Spectacle." Osprey Publishing, 2009.

Chapter 7: Festivals, Pageantry, and Sports:

Orme, Nicholas. "Medieval Children." Yale University Press, 2001.

Cartwright, Jane. "The Sixteenth Century." Oxford University Press, 2002.

Knapton, Michael. "The Tudors: The Kings and Queens of England's Golden Age." Thomas Dunne Books, 2011.

Conclusion:

Guttmann, Allen. "From Ritual to Record: The Nature of Modern Sports." Columbia University Press, 1978.

Elias, Norbert. "The Quest for Excitement: Sport and Leisure in the Civilizing Process." Blackwell, 1986.

Poliakoff, Michael B. "Sport in the Greek and Roman Worlds." Oxford University Press, 1997.

www.ingramcontent.com/pod-product-compliance
Lightning Source LLC
LaVergne TN
LVHW012119070526
838202LV00056B/5793